A book is like a GARDEN carried in the pocket.

– Chinese Proverb

The story of the three Lok brothers began when their parents immigrated to Hong Kong from China in the 1950s. with them growing up in Hong Kong.
The three brothers include Kevin, David, and Ed, all of whom were named after the Chinese saying, "Four Pillars to Build a Country."

These four pillars are Courtesy, Responsibility, Integrity, and Shame. The three brothers' father and an uncle married two sisters. The eldest male cousin received the name of "Li", which means Courtesy. The eldest brother David, was given the name "Yee", which means Responsibility. Kevin Lok was given the name "Lim", which means Integrity. Ed was named "Leung", which means Pillar. All of the Lok families are currently residing in California, Illinois, and Ohio.

Betty Lok is married to Kevin, and both are grateful to Richard Wong, Kevin's childhood friend who resides in Hong Kong, for his valued contribution and translations used in this book.

The First Pillar

COURTESY

沈默是金

– Silence is Golden

Listen before you speak.
A smart one will listen, while a
fool claims to already know.

不看僧面 看佛面

(Nice to the monk, for the sake of Buddha)

Be nice to people, for they have connection to someone that we care about.

倒屣相迎

(Quick to welcome a visitor; the host forgets to put on shoes.)

Be a good host for all visitors to your home.

以德報怨

(Return hurts with kindness.)

Love conquers everything. Treat those who've wronged you with love.

好心有好報

(A good heart will have good return.)

One who treats people kindly, will be treated kindly.

The First Pillar

COURTESY

一言既出 駟馬難追

(Once a word out of our mouth, we can't take it back even with the fastest horse.)

Use your words wisely. It's hard to take back words once they've been said.

助人為快 樂之本

(Helping people is the basis of happiness.)

It is better to be a giver than a taker.

投鼠忌器

– *Do not throw expensive china to kill a mouse*

Beware of the consequences of an action before a fight.

雷聲大
雨點小

– Plenty of thunder, but no rain.

Don't claim more than what you can deliver.

The Second Pillar
JUSTICE + FAIRNESS IN WORK

好天收埋
落雨柴

– Collect more wood on a sunny day to prepare for a rainy day.

When the opportunity knocks on your door, do your best with it. It may never come again.

JUSTICE + FAIRNESS IN WORK

一將功成 萬骨枯

(The glory of a general is built on thousands of his solders' death.)

The price for success can sometimes be too great.

斧底抽薪

(Cooking with a wok starts first with controlling the firewood.)

To solve a problem, it is wise to find the root cause of the problem.

兄弟同心 其利斷金

(If brothers put their minds together, their sharpness can cut through metal.)

Team work can achieve great accomplishments.

狐假虎威

– The Wolf pretends to be as strong as a tiger.

...'t abuse your superiors' power for your own gain.

本末倒置

– Don't put the wagon before the horse

It is important to follow directions and do things in the right order.

JUSTICE + FAIRNESS IN WORK

愚公移山

(A determined person is able to relocate a hill by their hands.)

Persistence is the key to success. If we pour our heart into the work, we can accomplish anything we want.

一將功成 萬骨枯

(The glory of a general is built on thousands of his solders' death.)

The price for success can sometimes be too great.

斧底抽薪

(Cooking with a wok starts first with controlling the firewood.)

To solve a problem, it is wise to find the root cause of the problem.

JUSTICE + FAIRNESS IN WORK

聽老婆話 會發達

(Listen to your wife, if you want to be rich.)

Your partner is the best adviser in our life.

一曝十寒

(A plant grows well with sunny days, then freezes during the cold.)

Short bursts of effort won't yield great results. Good work requires endurance.

一寸光陰 一寸金 寸金難買

(An inch of time is worth more than an inch of gold.)

Time is priceless. Opportunity is more valuable than money.

逆境自強

(Adversity is the best driving force to success)
Difficulty forces us put our act together.

利令智昏

(Wealth changes people.)
When we value money more than righteousness,
our character will be corrupted.

丁財兩旺

(Both people and fortune are of great value)
Try to accomplish goals in all aspects. Spending time with family is as
important as making money.

飲鴆止渴

(Drinking poison to quench one's thirst.)
When we rush, we can make bad choices.

The Third Pillar
INTEGRITY + CHARACTER

13

四海之内
皆兄弟

*– In the four seas,
everyone is our brother.*

Be friends with those of
unimportant and humble status.

死雞撐飯
蓋

— Chicken in a cooker keeps pushing up the lid

Accept your mistakes and learn from them. Deny your mistakes and you'll see them again.

The Third Pillar
INTEGRITY + CHARACTER

百折不撓

(Don't give up after one hundred repeated set- backs.)
Learn from mistakes. Keep going.

早睡早起 身體好

(Going to bed early and waking up early keeps you healthy.)
It is a healthy habit to go to bed early and wake up early.

聞雞起舞

(Wake up when the rooster crows and practice with the sword.)
Be happy, live a full life. Wake up everyday and enjoy the opportunities given.

INTEGRITY + CHARACTER

知足常樂

(Satisfaction makes happiness)

Happiness is being grateful for what we have.

人心不足 蛇吞象

(Greed is a snake trying to swallow an elephant.)

Greed is endlessly destructive.

The Fourth Pillar
HONOR

落井下石

(When someone is in a well, do not throw a rock into the well.)
When someone is in trouble, fueling the crisis is an evil act.

知錯能改 善莫大焉

(Recognize your mistakes, its never too late to do right.)
Know your mistakes and work hard to correct them.

愛屋及烏

(Love your family and anything in the house.)
Love our family. To have fulfilling relationships we must invest our time,
money and energy for our loved ones.

完璧歸趙

– *Returning jade to the rightful owner*

Be self-righteousness. One who has wisdom, courage and empathy will give up anything to do what is right for others.

19

The Fourth Pillar
HONOR

好馬不吃 回頭草

(A good horse doesn't turn back to graze the same grass.)

Never go back to something or someone who breaks our heart.

言出必行

(We must do what we say.)

Honor the promises you make.

一言九鼎

(Each word based on fact.)

Speak the truth.

掩耳盜鈴

(A stubborn person covers one's ears while stealing an alarm bell.)

Don't lie to yourself for it is the same as lying to others.

The Fourth Pillar
HONOR

有志者事 竟成

(Strong vision leads to success.)

A great idea comes from passion and courage.

莫逆之交

(Friendship is more important and helpful to success than money.)

True friendship is priceless.

百事以孝 為先

(First rule of all good is honoring parents.)

Honoring our parents is of upmost importance.

SPECIAL THANKS TO

The Lok Family for their persistence in translation and meaning.

Layout & Coordination By

MOONEY (M) DESIGN

Illustrations By

Zach Heiser

www.ingramcontent.com/pod-product-compliance
Lightning Source LLC
Chambersburg PA
CBHW042112040426
42448CB00002B/237